The Nature Explorer's Sketchbook

For the Art of Your Discoveries

Jean Mackay

Look around.

Start in your own backyard or neighborhood park. Look up at the sky, down at the ground and all around you for interesting things in nature to learn about and draw. Take this sketchbook with you when you are outside or when you visit new places.

Be smart, stay safe.

Wear sunscreen and bug repellent when you are outside. Ticks are common in many areas, so be sure to check yourself for ticks when you come back indoors. Also remember to be respectful of wildlife. Stay a safe distance away from animals so that you don't frighten them or cause them to bite.

What to sketch:

- Trees
- Flowers
- Birds
- Reptiles and amphibians
- Insects
- Water
- Skies, clouds, weather
- Landscapes

You can also add:

- Date and weather
- A list of wildlife you see
- Notes about what you find
- Your best discovery of the day
- Words to describe how you feel
- Poetry
- Things you want to remember
- Questions you have

After the rain
APRIL 23rd

Sugar maple

Let's get started.

The most important thing you need is your own curiosity. Take it with you always. You'll also need a pencil, pen, or markers and this sketchbook. You can also bring a few other art supplies to color your sketches.

Try This:

Draw your favorite art supplies and play around with them to see what kinds of lines and marks you can make.

11

What can you create with a pencil?

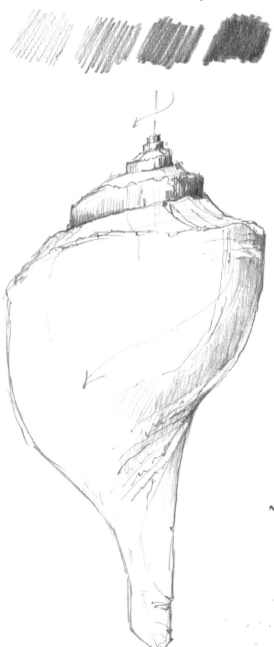

A pencil is a mighty drawing tool. When you pick up a pencil, you are using the same basic tool that artists and explorers have used for hundreds of years.

Pencils are perfect for lines and shading. Experiment with making different kinds of lines, from loose scribbles to precise shapes. Press harder when you want to get darker shades and ease up when you want lighter lines. Practice getting a range of light to dark shades with a pencil. This will help your drawings take shape.

beach finds

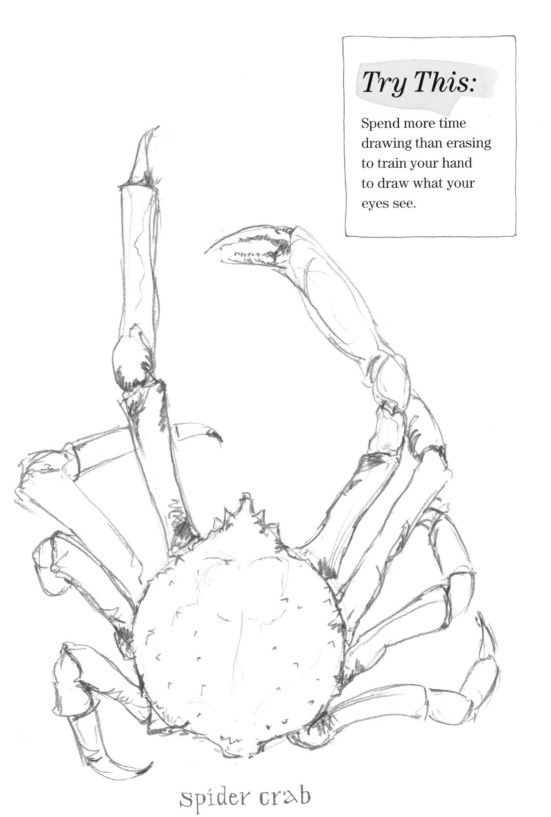

Try This:

Spend more time drawing than erasing to train your hand to draw what your eyes see.

spider crab

Bring your sketches to life with COLOR.

Have you ever seen the blue on the underside of a lizard? Or a bright red cardinal? Nature comes in a rainbow of colors and the more you look, the more you'll see.

You can add color with markers, colored pencils or watercolor paint. Sometimes, just a splash of color is all you need to bring your sketch to life.

Try This:

Use just a few colors when starting out. You can mix red, yellow, and blue to get all the other colors. Use a page in your sketchbook to play around with mixing colors.

Start with primary colors ⟶

mix 2

Color Play

add more water and see what happens

mix 3

15

Greens, Greens, Greens!

There are so many shades of green in nature. Take a closer look at just a few different leaves. Some are yellow-green, some more blue-green, some are dark green on top and light green underneath.

If you have a hard time finding the right colored pencil or green paint to match what you see, try adding a bit of blue or yellow and see what happens. You can mix different amounts of yellow and blue together to make many shades of green.

Try This:

Collect some leaves and try mixing greens to match them.

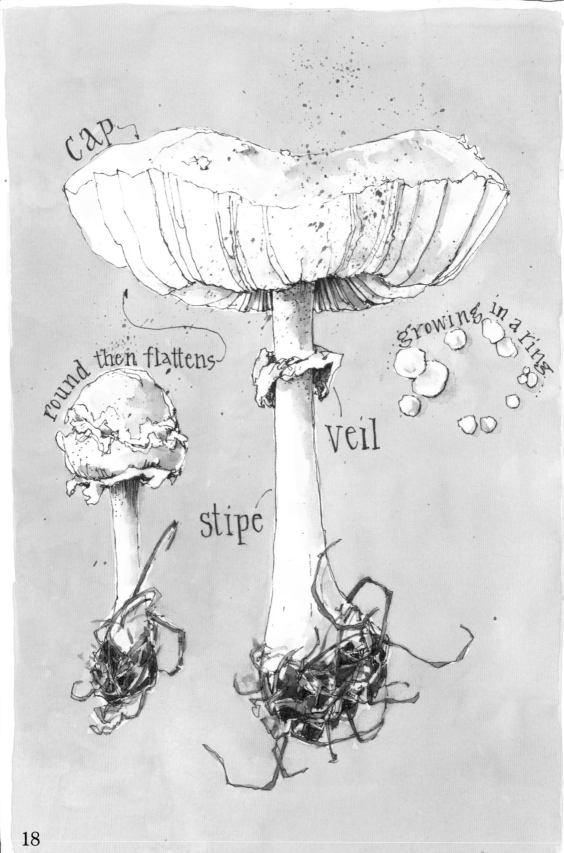

cap

round then flattens

growing in a ring

veil

stipe

Begin with one thing and see where it takes you.

There are many different ways to record what you see in your nature journal. The simplest is to draw only one thing, like a single mushroom, a seed from a tree, or a bird. You can try drawing your object from different angles. Or zoom in close on just one part. You can put several sketches right on the same page.

Another fun thing to do is to draw as many things as you can find that are related to each other. You can sketch everything at once or add new things to your collection page as you find them. Turn the page to see a sketch collection.

Try This:

Write down all the questions you have about what you are drawing. What are you curious about? Later, you can use the Internet or visit the library to look up the answers if you want.

cut in half

gills

Is it poisonous?

What kind of mushroom is this?

Does anything eat it?

Why is it growing here?

Tree Seeds

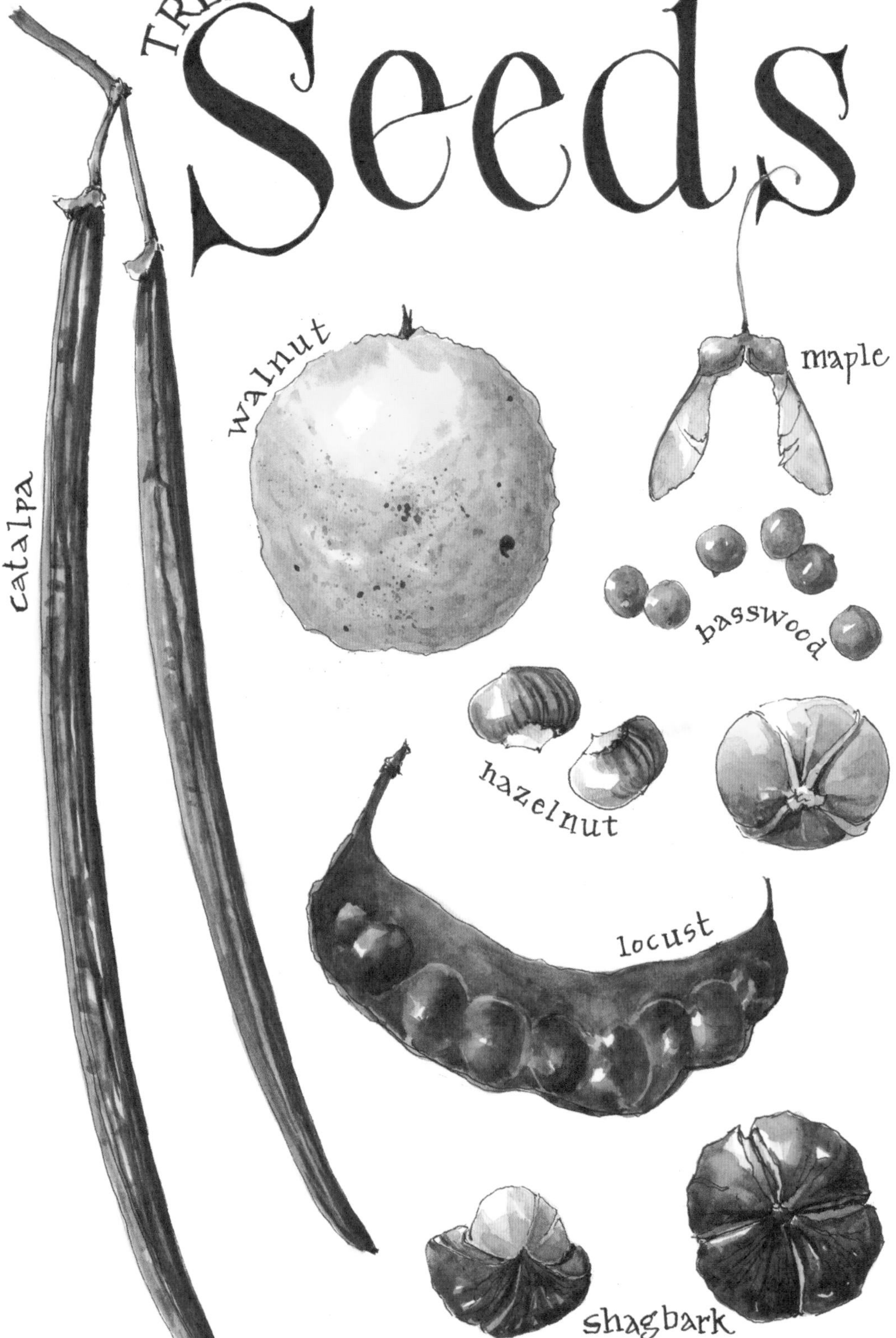

catalpa

walnut

maple

basswood

hazelnut

locust

shagbark
hickory

20

oak

sycamore

hophornbeam

dogwood

bitternut

jacaranda

eucalyptus

21

Record your journey.

Make a number of small sketches to record what you discover while on a hike or exploring in your own neighborhood.

START

lookout tower

BEAVER LAKE

MAY 24
63°F

goose nest

COLORS

deep lake

new grass

mud

buttercup

22 fern

blossom

sky

twig

SOUNDS

leaves crackling
wind blowing
CROWS calling
bees buzzing
geese honking
stream flowing

23

EXPLORERS

ARE

adventurous

curious

determined

respectful

prepared

eager to tackle
new challenges

observant

"The only failure would be not to explore at all."

...Earnest Shackleton
Antarctic Explorer...

Keep going.

Sometimes, it takes a long time for explorers to get where they want to go. They may get stuck or face unexpected difficulties. That may happen to you, too. You may have a hard time drawing something just the way you want to. Don't worry. Another important quality of explorers is that they keep on going. If you draw something you don't like, just turn the page and try again.

English explorer and naturalist Henry Walter Bates traveled through deep jungles and faced illness and homesickness during the 11 years he spent in the Amazon rainforest. He filled notebook after notebook with drawings of the insects he found from 1848 to 1862.

The world is yours !

The more you sketch, the more you will see and the better you will become at drawing. Keep looking. Keep exploring. The whole world is out there just waiting for you to discover it!

common milkweed

The Sketchbook

"Try this" activities...

Find grids to use on pages 34, 35, 54, 55, 60, 61 and 72, 73.

You can use pencils, markers, colored pencils, watercolor pencils, or a light wash of watercolor on the paper in this sketchbook. If you find that you really like using watercolors, you may want to try heavier paper that is especially made for use with watercolors.

Try This: Train Your Hands to Draw What Your Eyes See

Draw something without looking at the paper. Work slowly. No peeking! Your drawing may look a little crazy, but this will train you to really look closely.

Time yourself. What can you draw in 30 seconds? 1 minute? 3 minutes? You'll be surprised by how much you can record in a very quick sketch. Your lines will get better and better with practice.

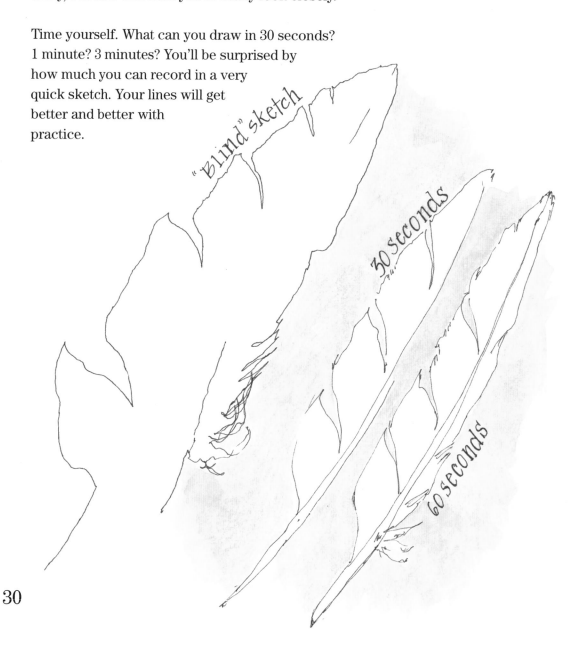

"Blind" sketch

30 seconds

60 seconds

34

Draw All the Insects You Can Find in 30 Minutes

Insects have three main body parts.

These parts look different in different insects, but they're always there.

head

thorax

abdomen

This is where the eyes and antennae are.

This is where the wings and legs attach.

This often looks like it is divided into different segments.

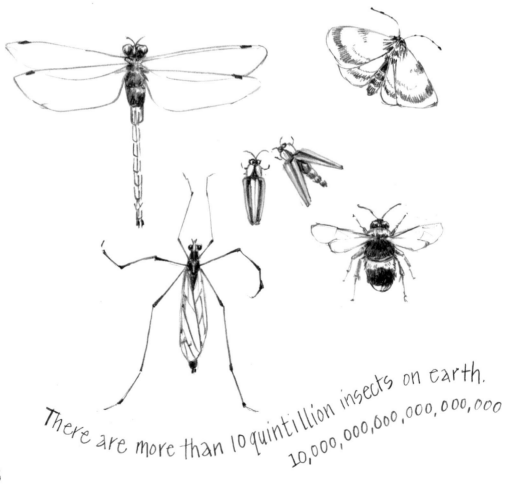

There are more than 10 quintillion insects on earth.
10,000,000,000,000,000,000

36

Try This: Make Your Own Trail Map

It's fun to make a map while hiking on a trail. Don't worry about making the map accurate. Instead, use it as a way to name and record the special things you find.

1. Mark a starting point for the beginning of the trail.
2. As you walk, look for interesting things that you can record. When you find something, make a small sketch and name the spot.
3. Move on until something else catches your attention. Give the place a name and make another sketch.
4. Make eight to ten stops and connect them with a dotted or dashed line for the path you walked.
5. Make a label for your map. Even if the place you hiked already has a name, you can give it one of your own.

You can make the map just for yourself, or to share with friends or family. Ask your family or friends to follow your path and try to find the things you drew.

SPRUCE ISLAND TRAIL

② Mossy garden

④ Decision point

① Whale Rock

③ fern alley

⑤ crow's overlook

⑦ monarch meadow

Start

⑥ squeeze trees

43

Try This: Take the Rainbow Challenge

Take a walk in your backyard, neighborhood, schoolyard, or park. Try to find all the colors of the rainbow. Make the color with colored pencil, paint, or markers. Label each color with the name of the thing you found. Next time, try drawing something for every color of the rainbow on a single sketchbook page.

columbine

mushroom

trout lily

moss

sky

water reflections

shadow on rocks

watercolor pencil

Spring walk in the Woods

54

Try This: Make a Collection

60

61

Try This: Sketch a Bird

Birds are hard to draw because they move so quickly. Just when you get started, they fly away! Here's one way to simplify birds so that you can sketch them more easily. Use a photo or a real bird for a reference.

1. Start with a line for the body that shows how the bird is sitting-- diagonal (slanted up or down) or vertical.

2. Add a half or full circle for the body.

3. Add a round head shape, tucked into the body. Notice which way the beak is pointing and make a line to show the beak.

4. Now add wings and a tail.

5. Always leave a little bit of white on the eye. This "eye shine" will make your bird look alive.

Try This: Add Some Fun Elements to Your Sketchbook Pages

DATE and WEATHER

70°F

windy!

JUNE 25

JULY 10th

AUGUST 31

snow

YOUR BEST DISCOVERY OF THE DAY...

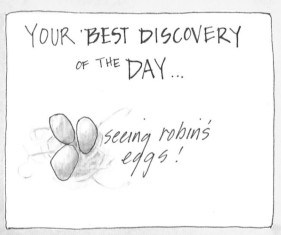

seeing robin's eggs!

BIG WORDS TO DESCRIBE WHAT YOU SEE OR FEEL

Wild

Cold!

amazing !!

YOUR OWN SPECIAL SYMBOL or SIGNATURE

73

Sketch one thing and write down as many questions as you can about it.